PRAYER

CHANGES

THINGS

Chapters 1-14 are guided prayers to usher you into the presence of God Yahweh to allow you to pour your heart out to him.

The LORD is near to all who call on him, to all who call on him in truth. Psalms 145:18

PRAYER

CHANGES

THINGS

Prayer Changes Things

Copyright © 2023 by Dr. Jamie T. Pleasant; Ph.D.

Biblion Publishing LLC

All rights reserved. No portion of this book may be reproduced, stored in a retrieval system or transmitted in any form or by any means — electronic, mechanical, photocopy, recording or other without the prior written authorization of the author — except for a brief quotation in printed reviews. Unless otherwise indicated, scripture quotations are taken from the Holy Bible, especially, the New International Version, New Living Translation, King James Version and English Standard Version.

First Edition / First Printing

Prayer Changes Things

Are you ready to experience change in your life? Are you ready to possess peace and prosperity like never before? Do you want to walk in all of the promises that God has ordained for you to have? Are you ready to occupy a permanent place of tranquility and joy in everyday life? If you answered yes to any of these questions, this book is for you! *"Prayer Changes Things",* will take you on a journey to realize the peace, prosperity and joy that God has ordained for you to walk in right now! Each chapter presents a personal prayer guide and answers from God Yahweh to help you reach new levels of fulfillment in your life!

Dedication

To my daddy, Anthony T. Pleasant, who was a perfect example to me of a real man. To my mother, Bertha Pleasant, who made sure I was financially prepared for life. What exceptional parents you were to me! To my wife Kimberly, whom I love dearly. To my children; Christian, Zion, and Nacara.

To Dr. Silvanus Udoka. I thank you from the depths of my heart for seeing in me what others refused to acknowledge. You sparked a flame in me that will forever burn for excellence and advancement!

Humbly Yours in Christ,

Apostle Jamie T. Pleasant

Getting the most out of "Prayer Changes Things"

Congratulations on purchasing this book! Get ready to achieve a new level of peace, prosperity, and joy through this helpful prayer resource. This book contains multiple chapters of daily prayers that will guide you into a deeper revelation of experiencing God Yahweh's desire for you to possess peace, prosperity, and joy in your life as you converse with Him and listen to His words of wisdom through answered prayer!

Psalm 34:4 NLT

I prayed to the LORD, and he answered me. He freed me from all my fears.

Table of Contents

Chapter 1	I'm Hurting Lord, Please Give Me Relief	13
Chapter 2	Give Me Peace, in the Midst of This Storm	17
Chapter 3	Help Me Move Forward	21
Chapter 4	I Just Want to Rest	25
Chapter 5	I Feel So Alone	29
Chapter 6	Nothing Seems to be Going Right for Me!	33
Chapter 7	I Feel My Help Coming!	39
Chapter 8	I Want To Seek You, So That My Blessings Can Find Me	45
Chapter 9	I Want What You Desire For Me To Have	49
Chapter 10	Your Will Always Provide A Great And Joyful Path To Prosperity	53
Chapter 11	I Want To See All Of Your Goodness On This Side Of The Dirt	57
Chapter 12	I Want To Walk In Abundance	61
Chapter 13	Please Release Your Blessing Power That Is Within Me	65
Chapter 14	Please Show Me Your Plan For My Prosperity	69
Chapter 15	I Want You, To Want Me	75
Chapter 16	This Is How Much I Love You	83
Chapter 17	Why Don't You Trust Me?	91
Chapter 18	What Happened To Us?	99

Table of Contents (Cont'd)

Chapter 19	I've Got Big Plans For You!	107
Chapter 20	I Am Right Beside You	115
Chapter 21	I Really Care About You!	121
Chapter 22	Wait on Me, I am Working On Your Blessing!	129
Chapter 23	I Know You Don't Understand	137
Chapter 24	Get Real With Me!	145
Chapter 25	Let Me Show You All Of Me	153
Chapter 26	When You Hurt, I Hurt	161
Chapter 27	Let's Celebrate!	169
Chapter 28	If I Say It, It's Done!	177
Chapter 29	Take A Chance With Me!	185
Chapter 30	I Specialize In The Impossible	193

Chapter 1

I'm Hurting Lord, Please Give Me Relief!

Heavenly Father Yahweh, I come to you in the name of your son Jesus and it is in the power of the Holy Spirit as heaven is opened that I ask you to give me relief from the pain I am experiencing right now. I am hurting deeply inside as I have experienced a loss in my life that is very hard for me to let go. This loss has me unable to function as I should and I am going in circles emotionally every single day. I want to get back to my normal self and experience the joy that I know you have for me. I trust you Jesus, but that doesn't take away the pain I am experiencing. Please help me Lord! Help me get back to being me and who you created me to be! I need you Lord! I need you now! I need your

Prayer Changes Things

comfort! I am pouring out my heart to you now as you are the only hope that I have left. Help me get back to experiencing peace and wholeness in my life. I believe in your word. I believe in your Son. I believe in your spirit and I believe in you and your healing power! This is my prayer and petition to you daddy Yahweh.

In Jesus' powerful name, Amen.

John 15:16-17 (ASV)

[16] And I will [m]pray the Father, and he shall give you another [g]Comforter, that he may be with you forever, [17] *even* the Spirit of truth: whom the world cannot receive; for it beholdeth him not, neither knoweth him: ye know him; for he abideth with you, and shall be in you.

Reflections and Thoughts

Write below what you feel in your heart God is saying to you concerning this prayer and any blessing you may have experienced.

Answered Prayer Journal

Chapter 2

Give Me Peace in the Midst of This Storm

Daddy Yahweh, in the power and presence of the Holy Spirit, I come to you in the name of Jesus. As heaven is opened, I want you to know that I am in the midst of a storm! My life seems to be out of balance and in turmoil. It seems as if trouble and persecution surround me on every side! I look everywhere to find encouragement and can't seem to find it anywhere. If it's not an unexpected expense, or a family situation, it's something that knocks me out of my peaceful state and into a state of being troubled and hard pressed. I can't seem to get my feet on solid ground. Every time I take one step forward, I seem to go backwards two or three steps. I have lost control of my life. I want to get control back! I want to get my joy back! I want my sense of wholeness and wellness back. I long to just bask in the presence of your peace and joy. Please help me Daddy Yahweh! Please hear my cry! Please bring me joy and wholeness again.

In the great name of Jesus who is the Christ, I pray, Amen.

Mark 4:39
[39] And he awoke and rebuked the wind and said to the sea, "Peace! Be still!" And the wind ceased, and there was a great calm.

Prayer Changes Things

Reflections and Thoughts

Write below what you feel in your heart God is saying to you concerning this prayer and any blessing you may have experienced.

Prayer Changes Things

Answered Prayer Journal

Chapter 3

Help Me Move Forward

Great God Yahweh, my dear daddy, it is in the Spirit that I come to your throne in the name of Christ Jesus as heaven is opened that I lay my burden on you in order for me to move forward with my life! I have been stuck in this space where I am unable to move forward with my life after suffering a setback that really has me down. I have always been able to bounce back from disappointment and things of that nature, but this one, has me really struggling. I need you to remove this burden from me that is weighing me and my relationship with you, my family and others down. I know that you are a burden bearer, heavy load sharer and yoke remover. Therefore, my God and my Lord, I need you now, more than ever before. I want to be free. I want to be strong. I want to be whole. Help me Daddy Yahweh, get my self-worth and esteem back, so that I am no longer sad and downtrodden. I am not happy being in this state of mind. It is not only affecting my mind, but also my body and my spirit. I want to experience wholeness and peace again. Jesus, I trust you. I need you. I implore you, please come and help me move forward and put the past behind me. I don't have time to look back because I can't afford to go back. I want to move forward.

Philippians 3:13-14

[13] Brothers, I do not consider that I have made it my own. But one thing I do: forgetting what lies behind and straining forward to what lies ahead, [14] I press on toward the goal for the prize of the upward call of God in Christ Jesus

Reflections and Thoughts

Write below what you feel in your heart God is saying to you concerning this prayer and any blessing you may have experienced.

_____

_____

_____

_____

_____

_____

_____

_____

_____

_____

_____

_____

_____

Prayer Changes Things

Answered Prayer Journal

Chapter 4

I Just Want to Rest

Jesus, it is through your name that I come to my, Daddy, God Yahweh. It is in the power of the Spirit, and as heaven is opened for me, I openly confess, that I need to rest. I am tired. I am heavy laden. I am deeply and heavily burdened. It seems as if the world is on my shoulders. I am worn down and I want to get a good night's sleep and wake up refreshed the next day. It's hard for me to wake up in the morning. It's just as hard for me to lay down and go to sleep at night. What a mess this is for me. I just want to relax and rest. When I am in bed, I just toss and turn. It seems as if I can't find a place of comfort or peace at night. I want to wake up with the excitement that I will experience joy and accomplish things that I never have before. I want to have the energy to not just make it through the day, but make each and every day, better than the day before. Daddy Yahweh, I want to rest in your loving arms! I want to rest in the bosom of your joy! I want to rest in the spirit of your being. Please Lord, help me rest! Give me rest! I need your rest. I am sharing with you from my heart, what I am going through. Now Lord, please take my concerns and in exchange, give me joy, strength and peace in its place as I release what I am going through to you. I want to just rest.

Matthew 11:28-29

[28] Come to me, all who labor and are heavy laden, and I will give you rest. [29] Take my yoke upon you, and learn from me, for I am gentle and lowly in heart, and you will find rest for your souls

Prayer Changes Things

Reflections and Thoughts

Write below what you feel in your heart God is saying to you concerning this prayer and any blessing you may have experienced.

Answered Prayer Journal

Chapter 5

I Feel So Alone

God Yahweh, it is in the name of Jesus, and it is through the Holy Spirit that I come to you as heaven is opened and ask you to allow me to express my loneliness to you. Often, it seems as if I am in this world all by myself. It seems that I am making it through this life without any help or concern from anyone else. Why am I feeling this way? Is there something that I am doing wrong? Why does it seem that no one wants to help me or contribute positively in my life when I need help? Lord, I have no one else to turn to but you. You said you would be with me and comfort me in all my times of need. Why can't I feel that from you now? Where are you Daddy? Where are you Christ? Holy Spirit, I need to feel your presence! Am I too busy? If so, I will change that.

Am I overlooking you reaching out to me? If so, I will give you my undivided attention from now on. Help me Lord! I don't like this feeling of loneliness. I want to experience your loving presence with me at all times. This is a very big world. It is too big for me to have to go through its challenges by myself. Please take away this loneliness. Please take away this emptiness. Walk with me Lord! Talk to me Lord! I am here and ready for a closer relationship with you.

Psalms 23:4

⁴Even though I walk through the valley of the shadow of death, I will fear no evil, for you are with me; your rod and your staff, they comfort me.

Hebrews 13:5b

…"I will never leave you nor forsake you.

Reflections and Thoughts

Write below what you feel in your heart God is saying to you concerning this prayer and any blessing you may have experienced.

Answered Prayer Journal

Chapter 6

Nothing Seems to be Going Right for Me!

It is in the Holy Spirit I come to you Father Yahweh, through Yeshua the Christ. Today I come to you because I need you to release your blessing power in me. Nothing seems to be going right for me. Everything seems to be falling apart in my life. It seems as though everything I touch, turns into a disaster. Bad news, seem to follow me wherever I am. Disaster and disruption surround me at all angles. Lord, I know you have the ability to provide for me without me ever having to ask you for anything. I know you can turn this around for me and give me peace in this area of my life. I know you know my thoughts before I even think them. You even think above and beyond what I can ever imagine. Therefore, I am releasing all of my disappointments, setbacks and tribulations, to you. I want you to release the ability for me to tap into your divine spiritual well of eternal provision. Lord, I am asking you to release that power in me that will allow me to go beyond any of my hardships and disappointments. What I am really saying Lord is that, I am surrendering my all to you, to care and provide for me and give me a life of victory and success. I am learning that the more I get in your presence to enjoy and obey you for who you are, the more you pour out blessings in my life that I can't even imagine in my mind. I am learning that in the midst of experiencing hardships and unpleasant challenges in my life, you are working them out for my betterment. Help me understand that trouble doesn't last always. Help me see a better day! Help me see a bigger you! I need you Lord Yahweh! Finally, Lord, I release that fountain that flows from you into my being that I can live eternally in peace and success through your son Jesus Christ! Work your power in my life! Work your power in my various situations! Work your power in my family! I pray for the working of this mighty power of yours on the inside of me. Thank you Lord. In Jesus' mighty name I pray, Amen.

Romans 8:28

[28] And we know that for those who love God all things work together for good, for those who are called according to his purpose.

Ephesians 3:20 (NIV)

[20]Now to him who is able to do immeasurably more than all we ask or imagine, according to his power that is at work within us,

Reflections and Thoughts

Write below what you feel in your heart God is saying to you concerning this prayer and any blessing you may have experienced.

_____

_____

_____

_____

_____

_____

_____

_____

_____

_____

_____

_____

_____

_____

Answered Prayer Journal

Prayer Changes Things

Chapter 7

I Feel My Help Coming!

In Christ Jesus, I come to you Daddy Yahweh in the Holy Spirit on this seventh day of my pursuit of peace through prayer. As heaven is opened, I want to thank you in advance for providing me with peace in my life. I want to thank you for helping me in these seven days to see and know that you are a loving God that cares for me. I know that you are always there for me. I know that you will always talk to me and guide me towards a path of peace and joy. I am going to do my best Father Yahweh, to remember that you are always here and ready to help me when I cry out to you. I am proclaiming to heaven and earth, that from now on, I will call on your name in times of heartache and trouble. I will pour my heart out to you in truth because I know you will hear me. I will bear my soul to you, and you only, as I know you are the source of my strength and the strength of my life. I can feel your help and my strength coming back. I am declaring and decreeing your greatness and the peace that you have brought back into my life. I further proclaim and profess that you, God Yahweh, along with your son Jesus and the Holy Spirit, will always have my back. You will never let me down or leave me alone to fight any battle in this life. All of my victories that I will experience in life belong to you, because all power and strength comes from you, for me to possess. I take possession of this peace now! I claim it as my own. Thank you Father Yahweh. I feel my help! I see my help! I welcome the presence of your help you have provided for me. I know it comes from you, God Yahweh, your Son Jesus and the Holy Spirit!

In Jesus' name, I pray thankfully for transforming me, Amen. Amen. And, Amen!

Psalms 121:1-2

¹ I lift up my eyes to the hills.
From where does my help come?
² My help comes from the LORD,
who made heaven and earth.

.

Psalms 46:1

¹ God is our refuge and strength,
a very present help in trouble.

Reflections and Thoughts

Write below what you feel in your heart God is saying to you concerning this prayer and any blessing you may have experienced.

_____

_____

_____

_____

_____

_____

_____

_____

_____

_____

_____

_____

_____

_____

Answered Prayer Journal

Chapter 8

I Want To Seek You, So That My Blessings Can Find Me!

Heavenly Father, I come to you in the name of your son Jesus and it is in the power of the Holy Spirit as heaven is opened that I ask you to give me the ability to understand that I must seek you and pursue you in order for all the things you have ever ordained for me to have, will manifest in my life! Lord, I seek your guidance and rulership in my life. I want to feel and sense your heartbeat, love and guidance in my daily walk with you. I pray that I can have the ability to understand your will for my life concerning the things you want me to do for you in your kingdom. I understand that it is only in your kingdom that I will find TRUE PROSPERITY that will bring me peace and joy. Therefore, Lord, I am asking you to give me a KINGDOM ASSIGNMENT and a desire to pursue it and I know that all other things in my life will fall into place. Your word says that material and spiritual things will follow me as I follow my purpose in your KINGDOM on my KINGDOM ASSIGNMENT! I believe this and receive it in the name of Jesus. I also know that the main key to my being able to prosper lies in my ability to function in your kingdom as I pursue and seek you with all my heart for your purposes that you pre-ordained on this earth for me to walk in. I'm ready Lord, SHOW ME YOUR KINGDOM and my ASSIGNMENT!

> *This day I pray that I will seek what you have planned for me to do for you that I may prosper!*

In Jesus' powerful name, Amen.

Matthew 6:33 (ESV)
[33] But seek first the kingdom of God and his righteousness, and all these things will be added to you.

Reflections

Write below what you feel in your heart God is saying to you concerning this prayer and any blessing you may have experienced.

_____

_____

_____

_____

_____

_____

_____

_____

_____

_____

_____

_____

_____

Chapter 9

I Want What You Desire For Me To Have

Daddy, in the power of the Holy Spirit, I come to you in the name of Jesus. As heaven is opened, I want you to know that I am ready for you to place your desires for my life in my heart. I want you to shape and mold my heart, soul and mind to conform to your desires. I know your desire for me is to have a blessed and stress-free life as I become a positive testimony to the world of your goodness. You know more about me, than I know about myself. In fact, I know that you desire what's best for me and I want your wisdom and direction to rule in my life as I walk in your blessings and prosperity according to your plan and purpose. Simply put Lord, I know that my greatest desire falls short of your planned blessings you have for me. Therefore, I seek that my heart can be transformed into the likeness of yours, so that I will never miss the best of what you have for my life. I only want what you desire for me to have God. I know that I am not LIMITING myself, but, by wanting what you desire for me, I am allowing myself to walk in UNLIMITED BLESSINGS and PROSPERITY from you.

> *This day I pray that your heart will become my heart and I desire what you desire for me!*

In His great name who is Jesus the Christ I pray, Amen.

Psalm 37:4 (ESV)
⁴Delight yourself in the LORD, and he will give you the desires of your heart.

Reflections

Write below what you feel in your heart God is saying to you concerning this prayer and any blessing you may have experienced.

Chapter 10

Your Will Always Provides a Great and Joyful Way To Prosperity!

My God, it is in the Spirit that I come to your throne in the name of Christ Jesus as heaven is opened and ask you today to show me your will for my life and the things you want me to accomplish and have. Lord, I pray that I may have the opportunity to experience how your will can open up a great and prosperous way for me. I know that in all things I should ask and seek your will in order that the way to the things I desire and want to accomplish will be opened for me to walk into with peace, joy and contentment. Help me understand how surrendering my will and what I think is the best PATH for me to take in obtaining something, is nowhere close to how accessible your blessing is for me upon me seeking your will. I want to experience how YOUR WILL is the best WAY I can ever take in pursuit of things and goals in my life. What a blessing it is to know that when I seek, accept and walk in your will, doors will open up to me that I never even knew existed. Oh, how I'm basking in your anointing knowing that doors will open for me that I can walk through without going through unnecessary heartache, pain and challenges. Oh, how I'm basking in the fact that your peace will go before me in whatever I do because your will is leading the way to my blessing! I now picture myself accomplishing things without being tired or drained! I can see myself doing things I never thought I could do. I can see myself resting at night in my bed knowing that you have me covered on all sides because your WILL has made a peaceful and joyful way for me. This is my prayer Lord, In Jesus' name, Amen.

> ***This day I pray that I will surrender my will to conform to your will so that your way will bring me to a place of peace, joy and contentment.***

Psalm 143:10 (ESV)

¹⁰Teach me to do your will, for you are my God! Let your good Spirit lead me on level ground!

Luke 22:41-42 (ESV)

⁴¹And he withdrew from them about a stone's throw, and knelt down and prayed, ⁴²saying, "Father, if you are willing, remove this cup from me. Nevertheless, not my will, but yours, be done."

Reflections

Write below what you feel in your heart God is saying to you concerning this prayer and any blessing you may have experienced.

_____

_____

_____

_____

_____

_____

_____

_____

_____

_____

_____

_____

_____

_____

Chapter 11

I Want To See All Of Your Goodness On This Side Of The Dirt!

Jesus, it is through you that I come to the Father in the power of the Spirit and as heaven is opened for me, I ask that you allow me to see all of your goodness while I am here on earth! Yes Lord, I want to experience all of the good things that you have ordained for me while I am on this earth. Lord, I know that heaven is a place full of joy, peace, love, goodness and your glory. I also know that heaven is a place you have ordained to be replicated right here on earth now! I know this because when you taught the disciples how to pray, you told them that your kingdom would come on earth as it is in heaven. Help me release heaven on

Prayer Changes Things

this earth in my life right now. I want to experience the best of heaven on earth before I die. I want to prosper in peace now! I want to prosper in joy now! I want to experience love and contentment right now! I want to live good, eat good and ride good! Yes Lord, I really want this type of life now. I want to dress good, feel good and talk good. I want to be able to bless others and do good for others right now! I know these are the things of life that you desire for mankind and I want to see them on this side of the dirt. I know what heaven will be like. I know what being in your presence is like. I know what being caught up in your Spirit is like. My heart's desire is to see all of your glory and goodness while I am still on this earth in all aspects of my life. Come and show this to me Lord. I beg you to let me see your goodness in all areas of my life. It is in the name of Jesus I pray, Amen.

> ***This day I pray that I may see your goodness on this earth just as it is in heaven!***

Psalm 27:13 (NIV)

¹³I am still confident of this: I will see the goodness of the LORD in the land of the living.

Reflections

Write below what you feel in your heart God is saying to you concerning this prayer and any blessing you may have experienced.

_____

_____

_____

_____

_____

_____

_____

_____

_____

_____

_____

_____

_____

_____

Chapter 12

I Want to Walk in Abundance!

God Yahweh, it is in the name of Jesus, and it is through the Holy Spirit that I come to you as heaven is opened and ask you to allow me to walk in abundance! I know that abundance means to have excess and plenty. I want to have an excessive life in you Lord! I don't want too just LIVE! I want to have a LIFE worth LIVING! I want to have abundant joy, love, and peace. I want to prosper in these areas of my life with excess. I want to be able to possess forgiveness, patience and understanding in abundance as well when it comes to people that I encounter. I know as I possess these abundant qualities, I will also walk in excess of other things in this life as well. Lord, I honestly don't want abundance just for me to boast and show off my stuff to others. I vow that I will use my material abundance to build your kingdom here on earth. I want to use my abundance to help my family members. I want to use my abundance to help my local church. I want to use my abundance to help whomever you place in my life to bless. I know that abundance is given to me so that I can give to others. This is what I want to do as I live on this earth Lord. Please hear my prayer this day. In the name above every name, who is Christ Jesus, Amen.

> ***This day I pray that you would give me abundance so that I can give to others.***

John 10:10 (ESV)

[10]The thief comes only to steal and kill and destroy. I came that they may have life and have it abundantly.

Reflections

Write below what you feel in your heart God is saying to you concerning this prayer and any blessing you may have experienced.

_____

_____

_____

_____

_____

_____

_____

_____

_____

_____

_____

_____

_____

_____

Chapter 13

Please Release Your Blessing Power That Is Within Me!

It is in the Holy Spirit I come to you Father, through Christ Jesus. Today I come to you because I need you to release your blessing power in me. Lord, I know you have the ability to provide for me without me ever having to ask you for anything. I know you know my thoughts before I even think them. You even think above and beyond what I can ever even imagine. Therefore, I am releasing all of my requests, thoughts, desires, hopes, dreams, etc. to you. I want you to release the ability for me to tap into your divine spiritual well of eternal provision. Lord, I am asking you to release that power in me that will allow you to go beyond any of my thoughts, dreams, desires and requests. What I am really saying Lord is that, I am surrendering my all to you, to care and provide for me and give me a life of abundance and prosperity. I am learning that the more I get in your presence to enjoy and obey you for who you are, the more you pour out blessings in my life that I can't even imagine in my mind. Lord, I release that fountain that flows from you into my being that I can live eternally in prosperity through your son Jesus Christ! Work your power in my life! Work your power in my circumstance! Work your power in my family! I pray for the working of this mighty power of yours on the inside of me. Thank you Lord. In Jesus' mighty name I pray, Amen.

> *This day I pray that you would work inside of me so that I can work outside of myself to obtain all of your stored-up blessings in my life!*

Ephesians 3:20 (NIV)

²⁰Now to him who is able to do immeasurably more than all we ask or imagine, according to his power that is at work within us,

Reflections

Write below what you feel in your heart God is saying to you concerning this prayer and any blessing you may have experienced.

_____

_____

_____

_____

_____

_____

_____

_____

_____

_____

_____

_____

_____

_____

_____

Chapter 14

Please Show Me Your Plan For My Prosperity!

In Christ Jesus, I come to you Daddy in the Holy Spirit on this seventh day of my prosperity prayer. As heaven is opened, I ask you to please show me the plan you have to prosper me! I know that you are a strategic God and you had a plan for my life before I was born. In fact, I know that you had a plan for me as you were creating me. I also know that you gave me the ability to complete your designed plan for my life. I am ready to obey you and spend time with you in order to see and understand the PROSPERITY PLAN you have for my life. Show it to me Lord! I will not run away from it. I will not second guess it. I will obey and begin to execute it. Your ways are above mine and I will take the steps necessary to obtain the prosperity plan you have ordained for me. I know that your plans are always good for me. I know that your plans will never bring harm to me. I know that your plans will encourage me to move into bigger and better things for your glory and your Kingdom. I vow to you Master, that I am ready to walk into your plan for my prosperity in this life. I know your desire is for me to prosper as I establish and fulfill my Kingdom assignment on this earth for you. Here I am Lord, send me! Send me to my assignment! Send me to those that need me! Send me to serve others. I will forever give you all the honor and glory. My hope is in nothing less than your sustaining hand that is stretched out for me to do your will on this earth. I am ready to receive your blessings in my life! I am ready to prosper! I am ready to soar to a new level of life! A life that walks, talks and flows in abundance! The abundance of your love, glory and provision are ever before me and I am ready to walk wholeheartedly in them. I love you Master. My life is in your hands. Guide me and direct me according to your plans. Lord, here I am! Send me! I am ready! In Jesus' name, Amen.

> ***Today I pray that your plan of prosperity will become a reality in my life right now!***

Jeremiah 29:11 (NIV)

[11]"For I know the plans I have for you," declares the LORD, "plans to prosper you and not to harm you, plans to give you hope and a future.

Reflections

Write below what you feel in your heart God is saying to you concerning this prayer and any blessing you may have experienced.

_____

_____

_____

_____

_____

_____

_____

_____

_____

_____

_____

_____

_____

_____

> **Chapters 15-30 are God Yahweh's answer to your prayers. Focus on His words of wisdom and comfort!**

I prayed to the LORD, and he answered me. He freed me from all my fears. Psalm 34:4 NLT

Chapter 15

I Want You To Want Me

Psalm 23:1-2 (NIV)
¹ The LORD is my shepherd, I shall not be in want. ² He makes me lie down in green pastures, he leads me beside quiet waters,

Dear Restless One:

I want you to know that there are times when you will put yourself in uncomfortable situations where you will become very uneasy and unstable. I want you to allow me to take control of your life and guide you into a peaceful place where you will find rest for your soul. Look at how I ministered to David. He was one of my most loyal servants and sometimes he would find himself in very uncomfortable situations. I don't want you to think bad of yourself, if you find yourself not being able to relax, rest and enjoy yourself sometimes. What I want you to do, is put your trust in me to guide you to a quiet place when everything around you seems to be falling apart. I want you to desire to be with me and to allow me to listen to your needs and wants and provide for you. Will you let me do that? I really want to show you how much I desire you, to desire me. I need your love as much as you need mine. I want you to learn what David learned, and that was, when things get out of control and become nerve wrecking, call on me and ask me to guide you to a peaceful and quiet place. I am the good shepherd and I know when you need to rest and when you need to get back into the everyday responsibilities of life. I want you to learn how to enjoy the journey so that you can prosper in the fullness of your blessing when you get to your destiny. I ask you and beg you to let me guide all aspects of your life. Let me take you to a place where nothing can harm you or hurt you. Let me take you to a place where there are no worries. Let me take you to a place where you don't have to try to keep up with someone or compete with anyone. Let me take you to a place where you can take a deep breath and exhale all the concerns of your life. Doesn't that sound great? I thought it would. Remember loved one, I will never leave you or forsake you. I want to show you how much I love you by showing you the very best and peaceful time you could ever have in your life. I want to be more than a shepherd to you. I want to be your friend. I want you to know that you are loved. I want you to know that I care for you. Come on, take my hand and let me lead you to a beautiful and peaceful place. Let me take you to paradise. Close your eyes, reach out your hand and wait for my touch. If you wait for a few seconds, you will feel the sensation of warmth in your hand. When you do, that will be me connecting with you. I will be connecting with your deepest joys, hurts, doubts and anything else that you may be experiencing. However, I don't want you to miss the most important thing here. You will be connecting with my peace, love, joy, understanding and power. When all of me connects with all of you, eternity will unfold itself into a beautiful bouquet of flowers that can't do anything but be admired and appreciated by all that watch the unfolding of our love for each other. Come on, let's go on a beautiful journey together beside the still and peaceful waters.

Yours Forever,

Yahweh-Shalom
The Lord is your peace (Isaiah 9:6)

Write your response to what you are feeling right now.

_____

Prayer Changes Things

_____

_____

_____

_____

_____

_____

What will you do from now on when you are facing un-nerving situations in your life?

_____

_____

_____

_____

_____

Prayer Changes Things

_____

_____

What should you do when you feel like God is reaching out to you and longs to make a connection in time with you?

_____

_____

_____

_____

_____

_____

What circumstance(s) have you faced in the past where you ran away from God rather than allowing Him to lead you to a better place where you would find peace?

_____

_____

_____

_____

_____

_____

How did you overcome your concerns and rested in His love for you that he wanted to show you?

_____

_____

Prayer Changes Things

Chapter 16

This Is How Much I Love You

Romans 8:38-39 (NIV)
For I am convinced that neither death nor life, neither angels nor demons, neither the present nor the future, nor any powers, neither height nor depth, nor anything else in all creation, _will be able to separate us from the love of God_ that is in Christ Jesus our Lord.

Dear Beloved Child:

Do you have any idea how much I love you? Do you know how much you mean to me? Look at what I told Paul to say to remind you of my love for you. Nothing can come between you and I. I am a loving Father and want you to know that I will not fall out of love with you. In fact, there is no evil principality, power, demon or even angel that can whisper in my ear or falsely accuse you and change my feelings about you. I loved you, before you loved yourself. I loved you, before you knew what love was. Why would I let someone come between us? I can't do that. It is not my nature. Stop doubting my love for you. When you fail, don't run and hide from me. Don't think that I will not listen to you or never give you another chance. Trust me and love me back. Let me know how much you love me. Write me a poem. Sing to me. Write me a letter. Talk to me when you are down. Let me know what is on your mind. I won't turn my back on you. I will listen to you and express my love to you. I am a loving Father that forgives and loves unconditionally. Nothing can separate me from you, based on how strongly I feel about you. Stop looking at me only as the God of everything. Start seeing me as your Father. See me as a loving, forgiving, understanding and patient Daddy. That's who I am.

That is who I want to become for you. I love you precious child. I really do. I love you with all my heart!

Your Daddy,

Yahweh-Eli
The Lord your God (Psalm 18:2)

Write your response to what you are feeling right now.

_____

_____

_____

_____

_____

_____

Prayer Changes Things

Prayer Changes Things

What can you do to make sure you never forget how much God loves you?

_____

_____

_____

_____

_____

_____

_____

_____

_____

Prayer Changes Things

What can you do to remind God that you love him?

What does love mean to you?

Chapter 17

Why Don't You Trust Me?

Proverbs 3:5-6 (NIV)
⁵ Trust in the Lord with all your heart and lean not on your own understanding;
⁶ in all your ways acknowledge him, and he will make your paths straight.

Dearest One:

You have no idea how I long for you to place all of your trust in me. I watch you as you try to go about your way doing things without asking me for help. I watch you struggle and experience setback after setback, because you have done something on your own without my guidance. How I wish you would bring your concerns and plans to me and let me advise and direct your steps. I have been around much longer than you have. I have seen more than you will ever see. I have even experienced more than you could ever experience. So, why do you continue to do things on your own without me beside you to make your path successful? What can I do to earn your trust? Why can't you get real with me and pour your heart out to me with all of your concerns? Do you not love me? Do you think I am old fashioned and have no place in your life? Do you still need me? Or, is it that I am not useful to you anymore? Well, your actions show me that you don't trust me. When you make a decision by yourself, it hurts me. It hurts me when I see you doing things that are not beneficial to your well-being. It hurts me because I know it will set you back. It hurts me because I know you will become frustrated. I remember how it hurt me when Adam and Eve chose to taste the fruit from the forbidden tree. I talked to them and told them what was best for them. They did not pay any attention to me and made a decision based on how they felt and the way they saw things. They thought they really didn't need to consult me, and look at what happened. They thought that their knowledge and understanding was enough, and that they didn't need my guidance or blessing. They were wrong and it took me a long time to make things right again. See, dear one, I want the best for you. I don't want to hold you back. I don't want to hold you down. I simply want the best for you. But, you have to trust me. You have to lean on me and not yourself. I birthed you to be able to show you how much I really care. Please, just trust me.

Love Always,

Yahweh-Rohi
The Lord your Shepherd (Psalm 23)

Write your response to what you are feeling right now.

Prayer Changes Things

Prayer Changes Things

What can you do to make sure you never forget to include God in your plans?

Prayer Changes Things

What can you do to show God that you trust him?

Prayer Changes Things

What does trust mean to you?

Prayer Changes Things

Chapter 18

What Happened To Us?

Deuteronomy 31:8 (NIV)
⁸…he will never leave you nor forsake you…

My Love:

What happened to us? I remember when we first met, and how you came to me with open arms. With love, you expressed your most inner thoughts to me. You would tell me any and everything. Do you remember how we used to chat, laugh and walk together? You couldn't wait to wake up and express your thoughts to me. You were not able to stay away from my house, especially on Sundays. You came early and stayed late. You would get excited and sometimes even dance with me. Now, you come around every now and then. You act as though you never knew me. You would hold my hand and you would proudly tell people how you felt and enjoyed my touch. Now, you seem so far way. It's as if we never had a relationship with each other. What happened to us? What went wrong? Tell me. I want to know because I want to change things. I want us to get back to where we used to be. Back in love. Back in peace. Back in joy. Where did those days go? I want them back again. See, child, I miss you. I need you in my life. I need to see your smiling face. I need to hold your hand. **<u>I NEED YOU DESPERATELY!</u>** Come back to me and I will welcome you. I remember how the Israelites left me and abandoned me for another. They forgot all about me. They put me on the back burner for a quick thrill that only lasted a short time. They forgot that I made them who they were. I chose to prosper them. I created them to be set apart from all others on Earth for my pleasure.

And, in a seconds notice, they walked away from me. Oh, how that hurt me. It really hurt me to the core. But, I am faithful and I am forgiving and I still love them. I have an everlasting love for you that can't be defined by any known dictionary. I have a love for you that will outlast time. I have a love for you that can't be compared to any living and breathing thing on this Earth. Give me another chance. Let me back into your life. I am a loving Father that wants to show His love to His child. Child of mine, I love you very much. I will never leave you or forsake you. I have an everlasting love for you that will never end. I am faithful when it comes to you. I just want you back. I want you to love me with all your heart. Will you come back to me?

Yours Truly,

Yahweh-Sel'i
The Lord your Rock (Psalm 18:2)

Prayer Changes Things

Write your response to what you are feeling right now.

_____

_____

_____

_____

_____

_____

_____

_____

_____

_____

_____

_____

_____

_____

_____

_____

What can you do to make sure God never feels like you turned your back on Him?

_____

_____

_____

_____

_____

_____

_____

_____

_____

_____

_____

What can you do to show that you are committed to God?

_____

_____

_____

_____

_____

Prayer Changes Things

_____

_____

_____

_____

_____

_____

_____

What is the difference in saying you love someone and showing them that you love them?

_____

_____

_____

Prayer Changes Things

Chapter 19

I've Got Big Plans For You!

Jeremiah 29:11 (NIV)
[11] For I know the plans I have for you," declares the LORD, "plans to prosper you and not to harm you, plans to give you hope and a future.

Cherished One:

I just wanted to write you a note to let you know that you are on my mind. I wanted you to know that I have some big plans for you. I want to make sure that you become everything that I ever intended you to be. You see, from the beginning of time, I had plans for all of my children. None of my children are the same. But, I have given each of my children special abilities and gifts to operate in blessings while fulfilling my purpose for their lives. I want you to know that my plans are plans that will prosper you and make you better. I take no joy in holding you back or seeing you suffer. All I ask of you is that you seek me and then follow my directions to the letter in order to walk in your prosperity. If you remember, I had plans for Abraham to become a great nation. Do you remember that? I told him in order to be blessed from all corners of the Earth, he had to leave his familiar surroundings and follow the path I would lay down for him daily. At first, he had some problems doing that. However, he soon got the hang of it and I was able to bless every single thing he touched. In order for you to be blessed, you must follow me and all the plans I lay out for you. You can't veer to the right or the left. You must stay on the straight course that I lay out for you. Please know that I don't prosper my loved ones in a way that one would expect. No! I usually bless and prosper in situations that seem disastrous and

Prayer Changes Things!

harmful to the human mind and eye. Listen closely, I want to share a big secret with you, my special one. The path may look like it is harmful. The path may look treacherous. The path may even look destructive. But, the truth is that, the plan will provide prosperity and blessings if you keep your feet firm and true to what I have promised you. Simply put, I want to make sure you trust me and my plans more than you fear people and their doubts. Yes, child of mine, I have big plans for you. Plans that you can't even imagine. Plans that you can't understand. Nevertheless, I will make sure to do all I can, to get you to walk in your blessings. I love you just that much. Now, would you please relax and let me birth my plans in you? I really have the best for you, ok? I can't wait to talk to you again soon,

Your loving Dad,

Yahweh-M'Kaddesh

Prayer Changes Things!

The Lord your Sanctifier (I Corinthians 1:30)

Write your response to what you are feeling right now.

_____

_____

_____

_____

_____

_____

_____

_____

_____

Prayer Changes Things!

What can you do to make sure you never miss God's plans?

Prayer Changes Things!

What can you do to stay on the path God has laid out for you?

Prayer Changes Things!

_____

_____

_____

_____

_____

_____

_____

_____

_____

What does the word *"plan"* mean to you?

_____

_____

Prayer Changes Things!

Chapter 20

I Am Right Beside You

Daniel 3:25 (NIV)
25 He said, "Look! I see four men walking around in the fire, unbound and unharmed, and the fourth looks like a son of the gods."

Precious One:

I was thinking of you and wanted you to know that you are never alone. I am always with you in tight spots that may make you feel uncomfortable. I want you to think back at how I helped the three Hebrew boys when they were in the fiery furnace. I love showing up in those kinds of circumstances. Yes! It was very hot in there but I knew you could handle it. Did you notice how I had my Son right beside them and never left their side? Did you see how I kept them from catching on fire? Did you notice that they didn't even smell like smoke when they came out? Guess what? I want to do the same thing for you. I want to do more than tell you that you are blessed. I want to do more than tell you that you are more than a conqueror. I want to get in there right with you. I want to stand by you. I want your enemy to look in and see that the hand of God is on you and nothing that they can do can ever harm you because of my strong love for you. Oh Yeah! I have a love for you that no flame can destroy. No demon can come between. No hater can stop. I am always with you and will never leave you as I stand with you in the middle of your trial. Now, isn't that good news? You are a child of a strong Father! I am a powerful Father! No one can mess with my child and not have to answer to me. I am always on time and full of power when I show up! So, let's go do something great together! Let's make a stand together! Let's make history together! I am with you and got your back!

Sincerely Yours,

Yahweh-'Immeku
The Lord that is with you (Judges 6:12)

Write your response to what you are feeling right now.

_____

_____

_____

_____

_____

_____

_____

What can you do to be assured that God is with you always?

_____

_____

_____

_____

_____

_____

What should you do when facing uncomfortable situations when you feel all alone?

_____

_____

_____

What circumstance have you faced in the past that made you wonder if God was with you?

Chapter 21

I Really Care About You!

Mark 4:38 (KJV)
^{38}……Master, carest thou not that we perish?

Dear Love:

Never doubt my love for you! I love you more than you will ever know. I know there are times when it seems like I am not around. However, I am always just a call away from you. I remember how I had the disciples on the boat with my Son on their way to the other side of the sea. I remember how He had a plan to teach them that they should never worry about anything as long as they knew that He was right beside them. I wanted them to know that when He invites someone to do something, there is nothing that can stop or destroy the plan He has already put in motion. I want you to understand that when I start something in your life, don't let distractions or sudden storms scare or stop you from going in the direction I am taking you. Loved one, if you will notice, they started asking Him if He really cared about them. They started asking Him if He had planned their demise. I tell you, He had a plan. He already knew what He wanted to do. He simply wanted them to learn how to act the way He would act when unexpected negative events might come up. I want you to notice where He was when the storm broke out. He was at the back of the boat sleeping. He was in the back of the boat in a blissful state of rest and peace. I want you to learn from this that you should never let a storm take you out of your blissful peace and state of rest where I have placed you. If I have asked you to do something, when a storm breaks out, rest! If I have commissioned you to complete an assignment, when a storm breaks out, rest! If I have called you to let me use you to build my kingdom while serving in your purpose, when a storm breaks out, rest! Never let a storm take you out of your blessing! Never! Notice how He awakened and commanded the wind and the sea to quiet down and be still. I want you to do what He did. Quiet your storm down and command it to be still and remain quiet. Tell your storm that you are a child of God. Let your storm know that I am with you and that you have the authority and have been commissioned to change the atmosphere. Let your storm know that you can change it, but it can't change you! Tell it to take a back seat to what I am doing in your life! Tell it to go somewhere else. Let it know that there is too much power and too many blessings where you are right now with me! I want you to walk as I walk. I want you to do as I do. I want you to be as I am. Remember, don't just ask what would I do. On the contrary, do what I am doing. Walk and act like the powerful person I created you to be. Become a victor! Become a champion! Become an overcomer! I always care about you and want you to never doubt that truth. If you trust me and call to me, I will always deliver and bless you. I really will. There may be times that you think I am not around. There may be times that you think I am busy doing other things. There may be times you may think I have other things on my mind. That is far from the truth. I am just relaxing in peace, preparing a plan for your deliverance. Isn't that awesome? Trust me, I really care about you, my precious jewel.

Yours Truly,

Yahweh-Shammah
The Lord of the Present (Hebrews 13:5)

Write your response to what you are feeling right now.

Prayer Changes Things!

Do you now have confidence that God cares about you? Explain, why or why not.

Prayer Changes Things!

What should you do when you feel like God doesn't care about your present condition?

Prayer Changes Things!

What circumstance have you faced in the past that made you wonder if God really cared about you?

_____

_____

_____

_____

_____

_____

How did you overcome those doubts and rest in His peace knowing He had a plan for your deliverance?

_____

_____

Prayer Changes Things!

Chapter 22

Wait On Me, I Am Working on Your Blessing!

Isaiah 40:31 (KJV)
31 But they that wait upon the LORD shall renew *their* strength; they shall mount up with wings as eagles; they shall run, and not be weary; *and* they shall walk, and not faint.

Dear Child:

I know that it's hard to wait on me. I understand that sometimes you want me to move and act as fast as possible. However, I want you to know that when it feels like I am not moving fast enough for you, I am actually working in the background on a blessing for you that you can't even see. Do you remember that time when you needed that money and it seemed like it was

Prayer Changes Things!

never going to come? Well, I want you to know that I was working double time in the background making sure you wouldn't lose the stuff that you had that the enemy was trying to take from you. Yes! I was making sure that the basic things you always had, would not be stolen by the evil one. I remember when you asked me for some money to get something. I knew you needed the money as soon as possible. I knew you had to have it or things wouldn't work out. However, I had to make sure that while you were seeking money for one thing, you weren't losing more important things in your life. Do you know that one time the evil one wanted to place cancer in your body and I had to really work to fight it and keep you healthy. I knew that all the money in the world wouldn't mean anything to you if you had been diagnosed with cancer. I had to focus all of my healing, love and deliverance on your body in order to keep you healthy. See, I am always working a blessing out in your life, even when it doesn't seem like it. I made sure that Isaiah would understand that if he would just wait on me and never quit hoping in me, I would come in his life and give him a newness of mind, body and spirit. I knew that this would place him in a position to be victorious at just the right time. Waiting on me, means that I am working out your blessing so that at just the right time, you will have all the strength and energy you need to enjoy and keep the blessing I give to you. See, I want you to enjoy my blessings and not be worn out or over burdened with them. I want you to know that the key to blessings in this life is not just getting things you want, but wanting them, and keeping them, after you get them! Yes! You have to pace yourself when it comes to blessings! You have to know how to enjoy your seasons of anticipation, contemplation, preparation and celebration. These seasons are part of my plan to develop your character, spirit and mind to experience all of the

Prayer Changes Things!

enjoyment that I want you to have in this life from me. So, please take the time and wait on me. Wait for me to give you the strength to keep your blessings. Just wait for me to give you the joy to bask in your blessings. Yes, wait for me, and you will never go wrong. I know what you need at just the right time. I love you.

With all my love,

Yahweh-Jireh
The Lord your Provider (Gen. 22:14)

Write your response to what you are feeling right now.

_____

_____

_____

Prayer Changes Things!

_____

_____

What type of attitude will you have from now on when you have to wait for God?

_____

_____

_____

_____

_____

What should you do when you feel like God is taking too long to answer you or do something for you?

Prayer Changes Things!

_____

_____

_____

_____

_____

_____

_____

What circumstance(s) have you faced in the past that made you wonder if God was ignoring you and had other things to do that were more important than what you were dealing with?

_____

_____

_____

Prayer Changes Things!

_____

_____

_____

_____

How did you overcome those concerns and rested in His promise that He was working in the background on a blessing for you?

_____

_____

_____

_____

_____

_____

Chapter 23

I know You Don't Understand

Isaiah 55:8 (NIV)
"For my thoughts are not your thoughts, neither are your ways my ways," declares the LORD.

Genesis 3:6 (NIV)
When the woman saw that the fruit of the tree _was good_ for food and pleasing to the eye, and also desirable for gaining wisdom, she took some and ate it. She also gave some to her husband, who was with her, and he ate it.

Dear Loved One:

I know there are things that are happening in your life that you don't understand. You are wondering why you didn't get that job that you really wanted and desired. You are wondering

Prayer Changes Things!

why you were not invited to that event you really wanted to go to. You are wondering why someone that you thought was a friend, turned their back on you and no longer talks to you. You may even be wondering if you could be a better parent, spouse or friend. There are many things that don't make sense to you sometimes, I know. However, I want you to know that I have done all these things for a reason. The reason I have allowed these things to happen to you, is to give you the very best of what I have for you and not just things you think are good for you. There is a difference in "good things" and "best things". "Good things" bring temporary happiness to you. "Good things" don't bring the fulfillment that I want you to have in your life. "Good things" will never satisfy your inner being. However, my "best things" will bring long term joy to you. My "best things" will satisfy you on a level like you have never experienced before. My "best things" will satisfy your inner being for all of eternity. Remember, that the next time things don't seem to work out your way, that I have a "best plan" for your life. I want to give you my best. I want you to have the best of everything. You don't need a "good man" or "good woman", you need a "best man" or "best woman". Don't settle for second bests or leftovers. Wait on the best that I have for you. Remember that in life there are many "good trees" that you can pick "good things" from. However, there is a better tree that contains all the "best things" that I have prepared for you. Wait and be patient and pick from the best. When you pick from the best, you will always pick a winner! You will always pick a blessing! You will always pick my desire for you. Now, my child, go and pick from the tree of life that which is the best for you and live in peace and joy.

Yours Forever,

Yahweh-Jireh

Prayer Changes Things!

The Lord your Provider (I John 4:9)

Write your response to what you are feeling right now.

_____

_____

_____

_____

_____

_____

_____

Were there times when you wondered what God was doing as you were turned down for that "good thing" in your life? If so, write below how you dealt with them.

Prayer Changes Things!

How will you deal with having to wait for God's best in the future?

Prayer Changes Things!

_____

_____

_____

What negative circumstance(s) have you faced in the past that made you wonder if God was playing games with you or getting you back for something you had done wrong?

_____

_____

_____

_____

_____

_____

Prayer Changes Things!

How did you overcome those concerns and waited for His best in your life. Write on one side of this paper on the lines, the "good thing(s)" that you wanted that you didn't get. Write on the other side the "best thing(s)" that he gave to you instead.

Prayer Changes Things!

Chapter 24

Get Real With Me!

1 Peter 5:7 (NIV)
⁷ Cast all your anxiety on him because he cares for you.

Dear Fearful One:

Why are you afraid of me? Why can't you tell me the truth about all that you are dealing with and going through? Why are you embarrassed to share your deepest, darkest secrets, fears and concerns with me? Do you think I will love you less? Do you think I will walk away from you? I know, you think I will not look at you the same after you open up to me and tell me everything? Listen to me, I know everything about you. I know more about you than you know about yourself. I know what you are going to do, before you do it. Ask Peter. My Son told him that he would deny Him three times and he swore he wouldn't do it, but he did. Yet, he was forgiven. I will forgive you too. I want you know that I don't want you to be anxious when you come to me and tell me what you are dealing with. I want you to know that the meaning of anxious is fear. And, I want you to know that you can't expect to get relief from your problems, issues and concerns from me if you don't cast all of them on my Son Jesus. You see loved one, casting means to place by throwing the entire thing on Him. You can't tell Him about half of your issues. You have to tell Him about all that you are dealing with. Don't expect to get relief from a bill if you don't tell Him the entire truth about how the bill became too much of a burden for you. Tell Him about the role you played in making it difficult for you to pay that bill. Don't tell Him about half of it, tell my Son about all of it! All I want you to do is be real with me by telling

Prayer Changes Things!

my Son everything. Don't hold anything back. Open up your heart to Him and dump it all out into His loving hands. Neither He nor I, will walk away from you. I will open up my heart to you and give you strength and courage to face your issues and concerns. I love those that are real with me and not afraid to tell me the truth about themselves. If you are a liar, tell me. I'll still love you. If you are a cheater, tell me. I will still love you. If you are a thief, tell me. I will still love you. In fact, the more truthful you are with me, the more I will show you my love. You can always come to me and tell me your deepest concerns. I love real people. Remember, I told Peter that he would deny my Son and he did. He then looked for him, found him and forgave him. He then, made him the first leader of the church in this world. Now if I can forgive and use him, you better believe I can forgive and use you. Also, once I forgive you, I will remember your sins, failures and faults no more. Come on, open up to me right now and share your most intimate thoughts with me. Share your evil thoughts with me. Tell me about all of the bad things that exist in your life. I can take it. I am God. I am here for you for all of eternity. I just want you to be real. That's real talk, from a real God.

Forever Forgiven,

Yahweh-Chatsahi
The Lord is Your Strength (Psalm 27:1)

Write your response to what you are feeling right now.

_____

_____

_____

_____

___

___

___

How will you approach God now when you are troubled or in a trying situation and seeking relief?

___

___

___

___

___

___

What should you do when you feel like God will not love you as much as He did before if you do something displeasing to Him?

_____

_____

_____

_____

_____

_____

What circumstance(s) have you faced in the past that made you wonder that if you really told God the truth, He would distance Himself from you?

_____

Prayer Changes Things!

_____

_____

_____

_____

_____

_____

How will you make sure you never stop telling God the truth about certain things that are embarrassing to you?

_____

_____

_____

_____

Prayer Changes Things!

_____

_____

Chapter 25

Let Me Show You All Of Me

Psalm 119:130 (NIV)
130 The unfolding of your words gives light; it gives understanding to the simple.

Dear Curious One:

Have you ever desired to get to know me on a more personal and intimate level? Do you want to know what gets me excited? Have you ever thought about the things that make me happy? Well, I want to share some things with you that I haven't shared with many. I want you to know the most intricate details about me. Are you ready? Ok. Here it goes. I am a God that loves to be loved. I am a God that loves to be in relationship with his people. I am a God that is looking for someone that loves me and is willing to partner with me in establishing my son's kingdom on Earth. I am a God that wants to help you obtain every blessing I have ever planned for you. Many wonder what is required to get to know me better. Well, I am ready to share the secret with you. All you have to do is take time and begin to seek me through the word. That is, the Bible. Now hold on a minute. I want you to just begin reading some passages of scripture and watch and see if I will not become a living reality to you. You can start anywhere in the bible that you like. I want to suggest that you isolate yourself from being easily distracted. I want you to plan a certain time of day, every day, when you come to me through the word of God. Now it will take a few moments, but, watch and see if after a little while you begin to experience a calmness and peace like you never have before. Watch and see if all of a sudden you start coming up with solutions to the problems you may be facing. Watch and see if you will not start dreaming dreams in the middle of reading scripture like you never have before. You will even begin to think thoughts that you never thought of before. Do you know what is happening when you begin to experience these things? I am revealing myself to you so that you can see all the things I designed you to do before you were ever born. There is no reality of greatness or purpose in your life until you become one with me and I with you. I want to show you myself and become one with you so that you can become an outward expression of my inner desire. That's right! I designed you to become a living reality of who I am. I want people with their natural eye to see the greatness that I have placed inside of you. When they see your greatness, it is just my greatness being expressed through you in human form. That's something to think about isn't it? I know it is. Now, you can't just come to me for a quick moment and expect to walk away with all the essence of who I am. No! You have to spend time with me to be able to become a full expression of my love. In fact, I very seldom show my inner self to those that don't have time to patiently wait until I can reveal the fullness of their destiny in time and space. Curious One, I want you understand that just like a rose petal that opens gradually over time until it reaches full blossom, only then can observers appreciate the fullness of its beauty. That is the same way it is when I am sharing myself with you. I want to slowly reveal portions of myself to you until one day you look up and there you are, ready to be observed by all, to see the fullness of your beauty in the kingdom of God. They will see my fullness expressed through you when they see your peace! They will see my fullness expressed through you when they see your joy! They will see my fullness expressed through you when they see your greatness and accomplishments. I want to show you all of me so you can show this world of doubters all of you as an outward expression of all of me. But, it can only happen through the unfolding of time. It can only happen through the unfolding of knowledge. It can only happen through the unfolding of my love. It can only happen through the unfolding of my word in your life. So, what are you waiting for? Go get the Bible and we can begin this journey together. Let me show you all of me. I love you so much. Take care, Curious One.

Yours in love,

Yahweh-Bara
The Lord your Creator (Isaiah 40:28)

Write your response to what you are feeling right now.

_____

_____

Prayer Changes Things

How will you approach God now when you feel like getting closer to Him or knowing Him better?

What should you do when you feel like God is distancing Himself from you?

_____

_____

_____

_____

_____

_____

What can you do more of in your Bible time to make sure you connect with God and become one with Him?

_____

_____

_____

___

___

___

___

How will you make sure you never miss God's presence and precious moments that He wants to spend with you to share more of Himself?

___

___

___

___

___

Chapter 26

When You Hurt, I Hurt

John 11:33-36 (NIV)
**33 When Jesus saw her weeping, and the Jews who had come along with her also weeping, he was deeply moved in spirit and troubled.
34 "Where have you laid him?" he asked.
"Come and see, Lord," they replied.
35 Jesus wept.
36 Then the Jews said, "See how he loved him!"**

To My Most Loved One:

I want you to know that when you hurt, I hurt also. Look at how my son, Jesus responded to Lazarus being dead. Look at how He felt the pain of Mary, Lazarus' sister. Always know that I feel what you feel. And, believe me, when I feel what you feel, I will do something about it. I take no pleasure in watching you go through hurt and pain. I wish you would never have to experience such things. However, as life is full of sin and negative events, there will be times when you will hurt. Do you remember when your feelings were hurt and when your heart was broken because of your breakup with your mate? Remember the time when you felt so bad that you didn't get the job, degree, car, home or promotion you wanted? I remember them. I was right there looking at you to the point that I became troubled and hurt just like you did. You cried, and I did too. You felt bad, and I did too. You were miserable, and I was miserable too. You may have even wondered if I were so hurt, why didn't I immediately do something about it. Well, the simple answer is, I had to let destiny take its course. Yes! There are times when unfortunate events that hurt you will occur in your life and I must stand back and let them happen. Please understand I will not allow anything to happen to you that will make you worst

Prayer Changes Things

---

off in your life or walk with Me. There are times unfortunate things will occur that will cause you to cry and want to quit life. Please know that I am experiencing these things along with you in order to get you to a better place in your life. Your destination is better than you ever imagined and this was the only way to get you there. Yes, my loved one, even when you lose a person close to you in death, I am working on something better to happen to you. Mary and her sister Martha had to experience their brother's death in order to see a bigger miracle, which was his resurrection. Now, I know that your loved ones that have died and are still dead, haven't come back to life yet. But, I want you to know that they may have died but I promise you that something or someone was resurrected! Yes! There is no death that does not produce a resurrection. At every funeral, someone is touched by death and will focus on Me and begin to direct their lives according to my will. You see, what

Jesus was showing Mary and Martha was that unless a seed falls to the ground, there is no chance for another life to grow. I want you to think a moment about a loved one close to you that has died. Now, think about how you or someone you know changed their lives significantly after that. A lot of times, that is how death works. Notice that Mary and Martha became very strong in their faith and love for Christ. Notice also, how all those other people watching became convinced that my Son loved Lazarus. What a beautiful thing the effects of that one death brought to that city that day. Please remember, there will be times when troubling situations occur in your life, but be assured that I am right beside you sharing in your pain and trouble. Never forget that I will provide a way of relief and growth to come out of all your trying times. In the future, promise Me that you will share all of your hurts with Me. Tell Me everything and I will draw closer to you than you can imagine. I want to share in your trials, so I can better celebrate with you in your triumphs! So, let's do this together. Let's walk through the fire, rain and sunshine together. I am an all weather God. I am with you through it all. I will never leave you nor forsake you. I promise. I love you.

Yahweh-Shalom
The Lord of Peace (Rom 8:31-35)

Write your response to what you are feeling right now.

_____

_____

_____

_____

_____

_____

Prayer Changes Things

_____

How will you approach God now when you feel troubled and confused about why unfortunate things are happening to you?

_____

_____

_____

_____

_____

_____

What should you do when you feel like God is not with you in trying times?

_____

Prayer Changes Things

What can you do more of to assure yourself that God feels your pain and is there to help you?

How will you assure God that He is the only One that you trust during trying times and uncomfortable situations?

Chapter 27

Let's Celebrate!

Luke 15:23 (NIV)
²³ Bring the fattened calf and kill it. Let's have a feast and celebrate.

Dear Reserved One:

I want you to begin to have more fun! Yes! I said it! I want you to begin to let your hair down. Take off your shoes, relax and celebrate. The message I want you to take away from this letter is to learn how to celebrate precious moments in your life and not let them slip away unnoticed. I love to celebrate and want my children to do the same. I really do. Remember when I had them celebrate the Passover? The Feast of Weeks? The Year of Jubilee? The Feast of Unleavened Bread? And, let's not forget the Sabbath? Do you see how I like to celebrate with my children? I want us to have a good time that is festive and life sustaining. Notice here how the father reacts to his disobedient son's return home. He doesn't scorn him or make him feel bad. He throws a big celebration to let everyone know that he is glad his son has returned home. I want you to begin to learn how to celebrate your mistakes that have turned into life lessons. I want you to not be so hard on yourself to the point that you become depressed and disengaged with others that mean so much to you. We all make mistakes. Only when we acknowledge our mistakes and the lessons that we have learned from them, can we be free to throw a big celebration. I want you to celebrate the little things that you take for granted that are really huge steps into becoming the mature person I designed you be. Don't just celebrate birthdays, anniversaries, holidays and graduations. I want you to start having big celebrations every time you get a promotion, earn an "A" on a paper, win a game, and get accepted into a club or organization. I want you to celebrate your children. I want you to celebrate when they score their first point or touchdown. Celebrate when they finish their first recital. Celebrate every grade report period when they earn "A's" and "B's". Celebrate! Celebrate when your friend gets a new car, house, clean bill of health or loses weight. Celebrate! Celebrate when you buy your first expensive watch, article of clothing or jewelry. Celebrate! I will be watching to see if you will begin to celebrate life. Also, and most importantly, celebrate Me! Yes. Celebrate me sustaining your life and taking care of you. Celebrate the fact that you have ever lasting life! Celebrate the truth that you are surrounded with the help of The Father, Son and the Holy Spirit! We are here for you and will help you at all times. Don't be a party pooper. Be the life of the party. And, when you celebrate, do it big. Call all your friends and let them know that you are celebrating something good that has happened in your life. Let them know of my goodness. Tell them about how many times that I have delivered you and sustained you. Tell them how I am always there for you when you need me. Tell them these things when you celebrate. Now, guess what? The most cherished time I love to celebrate with you is when you come to church. Yes that is the best celebration of the week. I love when we can get together and celebrate all the good things that have happened to you during the week. I love when we come together at church and share the trying times you have experienced but place your trust in me to take care of them. I love when we get together in church and touch and agree and cheer together. It is simply the best part of my week. I never miss it. I am always there in the sanctuary waiting on you to find me and come to me in truth and love. What a precious time we always have. By the way, when was the last time that you came to the place where we celebrate? Come on back. Don't be afraid, I'll fatten a cow and serve it up to you. I will have the best of everything laid out for you to enjoy. I will even speak into your life and tell you of all the great things to come. Great things, that will bring you strength and hope. We will sing some songs, talk to each other and enjoy each other's company. What are you waiting on? Come on back to the house. Come on back to the house of prayer. Come on back to the place where you belong.

Yours and waiting,

Yahweh-Sabaoth
The Lord of Hosts (I Sam 1:3)

Prayer Changes Things

Write your response to what you are feeling right now.

_____

_____

_____

_____

_____

_____

How will you approach God when you feel like celebrating?

_____

_____

What should you do when you feel like celebrating small things?

What can you do more of to assure yourself that you are not missing out on precious moments that you should be celebrating?

How will you make sure that you celebrate the right things to the fullest?

Chapter 28

If I Say It, It's Done!

Genesis 1:3 (NIV)
³ And God said, "Let there be light," and there was light.

Dear Doubtful One:

I want to let you know that whenever I say something to you, you can count on it happening. What have you heard me say to you lately? Can you even think of one thing? I am constantly trying to get your attention in order to let you know about the plans that I have for you. When I say something, it definitely shall be. Notice how Moses gives an account of how the Earth began. In the beginning, the earth was formless, empty, dark and without meaning. Pay attention to how I simply just speak and all of a sudden light appears from nowhere. I want to do the same thing in your life. I want to speak into your emptiness and bring fullness of joy to you. I want to speak into the formless places of your mind, body and spirit to bring structure, purpose and meaning into your life. I want to speak into the darkest areas of your life and provide light for you. Do you see what I am trying to do for you? I want to always bring light into your life. Whatever you may be facing, struggling with, or need help with, I am here to speak into your nothing and create something out of it. Only I can do that. No one else can take a person that is empty to become full of substance and meaning but me. No one else can take a person that can't form anything out of his/her life and make him/her become full of purpose and destiny. No one can take a person that is dark and filled with evil and shape him/her into a gentle beautiful light that shines into everyone's path to show his/her greatness. No one can do that but me. The more time you spend with me, the more light I will speak into you. You are nothing more than an expression of who I am. You truly express yourself to others when your light can shine. I have created every person to uniquely shine in this life. Some will have very bright lights and others will have soft lights that simply compliment their surroundings. Do you know the type of light that you are? In my presence, I will shape you and develop you into the divine light that I always intended you to become. You will go from being sad to being glad. You will go from being empty to being full. You will go from being shapeless into being a mighty person of substance and purpose. You see, every time that I can speak into your life, you become more alive. Just because you are breathing doesn't mean that you are alive! It is only when you can shine your presence into a dark, empty and meaningless situation, that you are alive. When I speak into your life, no trouble, challenge or uncomfortable situation will get the best of you. Those things will not suck the life out of you anymore. In fact, they will give you life because you now will be able to shine and show your power and strength. You will thrive on challenges, troubles and trials. So, I ask you, how are you doing? Are you living or just breathing? Are you thriving or dying at this thing called life? Let me speak into your being. Let me speak into your spirit, mind and body. If you will be still and let me speak into your life, you will begin to live a life that is full of all the best of everything that you could ever imagine. Remember, my words are spirit and they give life. They give life to those that will allow themselves to be shaped by me. If I can create a universe, I can create your destiny. If I can make a planet out of nothing, I can make you into something that is great. If you look back at Adam, I first imagined

Prayer Changes Things!

him in my mind. I then blew on the dirt and created a small dust storm. I then took my hands and formed him out of dust. But, he was still not alive. I had created him and shaped him but he did not breathe one single breath. However, when I breathed into his nostrils the breath of life, he became a living soul. Have you not heard that all scripture is God breathed in second Timothy chapter three verse sixteen? Have you ever seen that? Well, you should go there and spend some time in my word. Then, you will see that no one can live without scripture breathed into their bodies every day. So, start living and not just existing. Go to my word in the Bible and let me breathe life into you. I want to speak into your life. I want to tell you something that you never ever thought would happen to you. I want to show you your future. And, remember, if I say it, it will happen. Open up your mouth and nose and take a deep breath. I love you!

Prayer Changes Things!

Love Always,

Yahweh-Bara
The Lord, your Creator (Isaiah 40:28)

Write your response to what you are feeling right now.

_____

_____

_____

_____

_____

_____

How will you approach God when you are perplexed and or confused?

Prayer Changes Things!

_____

_____

_____

_____

_____

_____

How will you view yourself when facing challenges from now on?

_____

_____

_____

_____

Prayer Changes Things!

_____

_____

_____

What can you do to assure yourself that you can handle all uncomfortable and challenging situations in your life?

_____

_____

_____

_____

Chapter 29

Take A Chance With Me!

Matthew 14:28-29 (NIV)
28 "Lord, if it's you," Peter replied, "tell me to come to you on the water." 29 "Come," he said. Then Peter got down out of the boat, walked on the water and came toward Jesus.

Dear Fearful One:

I want you to take a chance with me and do something you have never done before. The reason I want you to do something you have never done, is so I can give you something you've never had before. Yes! I want to begin a new adventure that I promise will only prosper you and elevate you to a new level in your life. Look at how I did it with Peter. I always admired him because he was never afraid to take a chance with my Son and I. There are many that associate themselves with Me, but never take a chance with Me. I have always wondered how someone can say that they are connected with Me and yet never do anything radical for Me. Did you understand that my child? Do you see what I am saying? I can't understand how someone can be around Me all day, pray to Me, praise Me, claim to know Me and yet, never try to do one supernatural thing in his/her entire lives. That is why I chose Peter to be the first leader of my Son's church. I knew he would never be afraid to push the button and do new things in the kingdom for Me. What kind of person are you my child? Can I select and trust you to depend on Me and get out of your comfort zone of normalcy and do something radical? Will you take a chance with Me to change your life? Will you allow Me to go ahead of you and prepare a new path for you that will only bring you to a better place, with better things, for a better relationship with Me, that will yield a better life for you? Will you let Me do that? I am waiting on you loved one. If you don't know how to do this, let Me help. Just come to Me and begin to talk with Me and each day I will begin to strengthen you to the point that you will start dreaming new dreams, thinking new thoughts, talking a new talk, walking a new walk and planning new plans. I promise you that after you start experiencing these things, you will soon find yourself stepping into something new that will change your life. I want you to be watchful of what I am doing in your life. I don't want you to get ahead of Me, but to watch Me. Did you hear Me? Be watchful of Me and wait on Me to invite you to get out of your normal life so you can step into a new and more powerful life. Be watchful of where I am and what I am doing at all times. Never take your eyes off of Me. You can't do that unless you are in constant communication with Me and understand all aspects of Me. So, what are you waiting on? What are you afraid of? What's holding you back? Come on and step out on the water and take on a new adventure to a better life and relationship with me. I want you to accomplish those things you have been fearful of. I want you to have everything that I ever dreamed of you having. Come on, get out of the boat and walk on the water and get your, house, car, healing, confidence, peace, love, forgiveness, boldness, job and everything else you need. I am here waiting for you to take a chance with me.

Love Ya,

Yahweh-Hoshe'ah
The Lord that saves (Psalm 20:9)

Write your response to what you are feeling right now.

Prayer Changes Things

_____

_____

_____

_____

_____

_____

How will you approach God when you feel the urge to leave your comfort zone and do something new?

_____

_____

_____

_____

How will you make sure you don't get ahead of God when venturing out into something new?

What can you do to assure yourself that you have the courage and strength to step into a new life with God?

Prayer Changes Things

Chapter 30

I Specialize In The Impossible

Daniel 3:22 (NIV)
²² The king's command was so urgent and the furnace so hot that the flames of the fire killed the soldiers who took up Shadrach, Meshach and Abednego,

Dear Love One:

I've saved this last letter for you and hope it's a blessing to you. It is so important, that I had to use the Hebrew boys example again. I want you to know that with me, all things are possible because only I can perform the impossible. Through you, I will do before the eyes of others, what they never thought could be done. There will be times when you will find yourself in some impossible positions where it seems like you are not going to make it. Be patient and faithful to me because I am setting up a scene for all to see my ability to deliver you out of impossible situations. I want you to know that I will always get you out of any bad situation even if you don't think I will. It might seem hopeless, over and disastrous. But, I have a plan to make you come out smelling like a rose and others will not be able to do anything but bow down and acknowledge me as the Most High God. Besides me, there is truly no other God. I am the Real McCoy. The One and Only. The Real Deal. I am the only God that can bring you into a better place after you were in a trying place. I want you to look at the three Hebrew boys. They were being tested by me to see if they would stand up for what they believed in. I wanted to test them to see if they would crack under pressure, forget or forsake me. As you know, they didn't show any fear when they were thrown into the fiery furnace. If you read the scripture in more detail, you will see that the king ordered the furnace's temperature to

Prayer Changes Things

be turned up seven times hotter than normal. You will also read that those soldiers who were ordered to turn it up, burned up and died as they were trying to place the three Hebrew boys in the fire. You see, I had already done the impossible even before they went in the fire. If the soldiers died just by getting next to it, how in the world could the three Hebrew boys survive after being placed in it? Well it is very simple. The lesson I want you to learn here is that there are some things that I have ordained you to be able to go through that others can't go through! You see, I have prepared an impossible situation uniquely for you, that only I can make possible for you to go into and come out of, stronger in the end. Make sure you are in your unique and impossible situation and you will definitely come out smelling like a rose. Also, look at how things ended up for them. The king couldn't believe that they hadn't died, so he looked in and did a head count and came up with four people alive in the furnace. You see, I allowed him to see the revelation of my Son in there with them. I am always beside you working out impossible situations. I am always beside you in your defense. Never, ever, forget that. Whenever you think you are alone, I'm right there! Whenever you think it's over and you won't make it, I'm right there. Whenever you think you are not going to survive, I'm right there. Yes! I am right there making the impossible, possible. So I have a request of you right now. I wish you will do it for me. I want you to take a second where you are right now and begin to give me praise! I want you to bless me right where you are right now. Will you give me a shout? Will you lift up your hands? Will you call out my name? I hope you will. If so, it will allow me to work the impossible out of your life right now and usher you into a realm of unlimited possibilities. I'm working it out right now! All these things I have written.

From my heart to yours,

Yahweh-'Izoa Hakaboth

The Lord your God, Strong and Mighty (Ps 24:8)

Write your response to what you are feeling right now.

_____

_____

_____

_____

_____

_____

_____

How has this book of love letters from God helped you?

_____

_____

How will you make sure you let God deliver you from trying situations?

Prayer Changes Things

What can you do to assure yourself that God will never lead you into a hopeless situation without a plan to deliver you?

Epilogue

One of the best ways to experience purpose working in your life is for you to give your life to Christ Jesus. Repeat these simple words and it will be a done deal. Repeat the following: Lord Christ Jesus as of this very moment, I accept you as Lord and Savior of my life. I now give my life to you to be fashioned for your purpose and glory. Lord, all of these things that I have said, I honestly believe in my heart and have confessed with my mouth to you. I know now that I have received everlasting life based on the work that Christ has done and will continue to do in my life. Lord Christ, thank you for bringing me to this point of my life where I surrender my all to you. It is in the Holy Spirit through Christ Jesus, I say Amen.

Humbly Yours in Christ

Book Dr. Jamie Pleasant for a Speaking Engagement!

For speaking engagements, please contact Dr. Jamie T. Pleasant at admin@newzionchristianchurch.org or 678.845.7055

About the Author

Apostle Jamie T. Pleasant, Ph.D., a modern-day polymath, is the founder and Chief Executive Pastor of New Zion Christian Church in Suwanee, Georgia. He currently serves as the Dean of Graduate Education at Clark Atlanta University. He is also a tenured Full Professor of Marketing at Clark Atlanta University's School of Business. Notably, he is the first faculty member in the university's history to be accepted into Mensa International, the world's largest and oldest high IQ society for individuals who have scored in the 98th percentile or above on an intelligence test.

Dr. Pleasant is the first African American to graduate from the Georgia Institute of Technology (Georgia Tech) with a Ph.D. in Business Management with a concentration in Marketing, earning that degree in August 1999. He is a 2016 recipient of the "Lifetime Achievement Award" from former President Barack Obama for

About the Author

volunteer and community service. He was awarded the "Game Changer" Educator Award by Reverend Jesse Jackson at the 2019 Rainbow PUSH International Convention. He holds a bachelor's degree in physics from Benedict College in Columbia, South Carolina, Marketing Studies from Clemson University and an M.B.A. in Marketing from Clark Atlanta University.

Under his leadership, New Zion has grown from three members when it started in 1995 to well over 700 in weekly attendance, with a focus on economic and entrepreneurial development. God gave him the vision to establish a Biblically based economic development initiative for New Zion Christian Church. He remains at the pulse of the economic business sector. As a result, Apostle Pleasant is in constant demand to train, speak and teach others at all levels in ministry and the private sector about business and economic development across the country. He has created numerous innovative and industry leading ministerial, business and economic development classes and

About the Author

programs, along with SAT & PSAT prep courses for children ages 9-19. He founded The Financial Literacy Academy For Youth (FLAFY), where youth between the ages of 13-19 attend 12-week intense classes on financial money management principles. At the end of those 12 weeks, they receive a "Personal Finance" certificate of achievement. In 2015, he established The Young Leadership and Success Academy that teaches young people between the ages of 10-21 how to invest, make presentations and start and operate businesses. Other ministries he has pioneered include The Wealth Builders Investment Club (WBIC), which educates and allows members to actively invest in the stock market, along with the much-celebrated Institute of Entrepreneurship (IOE), where participants earn a certificate in entrepreneurship after three months of comprehensive training in all aspects of starting and owning a successful competitive business. The main goal and purpose of IOE is that each year one of the trained businesses will be awarded up to $10,000 startup money to ensure financial success.

About the Author

Apostle Pleasant has met with political officials such as former President Bill Clinton and Nelson Mandela. He has performed marriage ceremonies and counseled numerous celebrated personalities such as Usher Raymond, Terri Vaughn, and many others. Several gospel music artists have performed at the church, including Tiff Joy. Each year, Apostle Pleasant conducts chapel services for Clemson University's football team and is a spiritual and personal friend to its two-time national championship head coach, Dabo Swinney.

As a civil rights leader, he is a close aide to Reverend Jesse Jackson and serves on the Board of Directors of Rainbow PUSH Inc. (Atlanta) and Director of Education and Economics. He serves on the Board of Fellowship of Christian Athletes (Atlanta Urban) and after the Columbine High School shooting, he founded the National School Safety Advocacy Association. His latest foundations include the Young Entrepreneurship Program (YEP) and the African American Consumer Economic Rights (AACER).

About the Author

He has authored numerous books that include: *How to Release Your Blessings Through Service in Ministry, When Purpose is at Work, Proverbs for Prosperity, Unshakable Faith, A Seven Day Prayer Plan for Peace, A Seven Day Prayer Plan for Prosperity, Prayers That Open Heaven, The Making of a Man, Capturing and Keeping the Pastor's Heart, Powerful Prayers That Open Heaven, Advertising Principles: Daily Quotes for Daily Blessings, How to Effectively Reach African Americans in the 21st Century, A Marketing Model of Ethnic Consumer Behavior, The Importance of Subcultural Marketing, An Overview of Strategic Healthcare, Discover a New You: A 21 Day Journey to Uncovering Your Uniqueness, From My Heart To Yours: Love Letters From A Loving Father, I'm Just Sayin': Thoughts for Successful Living, Today's Apostle: Servants of God, Leading His People towards Unity and "You Have What It Takes".* Apostle Pleasant is a lifetime member of Alpha Phi Alpha Fraternity Inc. He is the humble husband of Kimberly Pleasant and the proud father of three children: Christian, Zion and Nacara.

FINI

BIBLION PUBLISHING

www.ingramcontent.com/pod-product-compliance
Lightning Source LLC
Chambersburg PA
CBHW041923160426
42813CB00105B/3450/J